A high-status timber-framed building built for a family of substance.

Wattle and Daub

Paula Sunshine

A Shire book

Published in 2006 by Shire Publications Ltd,
Cromwell House, Church Street, Princes Risborough,
Buckinghamshire HP27 9AA, UK.
(Website: www.shirebooks.co.uk)

Copyright © 2006 by Paula Sunshine.
First published 2006.
Shire Album 455. ISBN-10: 0 7478 0652 7;
ISBN-13: 978 0 7478 0652 3.
Paula Sunshine is hereby identified as the author of this
work in accordance with Section 77 of the Copyright,
Designs and Patents Act 1988.

British Library Cataloguing in Publication Data:
Sunshine, Paula
Wattle and daub. – (Shire album; 455)
1. Wooden-frame buildings – Great Britain – History
2. Building, Clay – Great Britain – History
3. Wooden-frame buildings – Great Britain – Design and
construction
I. Title 721'.0448'0942
ISBN-13: 978 0 7478 0652 3
ISBN-10: 0 7478 0652 7.

Front cover: (Clockwise from top left) Woven wattles and ancient daub to be repaired. The author tying wattles. A green oak structure with wattle and daub infill, erected in 2003. Poplar Cottage at the Weald & Downland Open Air Museum, Singleton, West Sussex.

ACKNOWLEDGEMENTS
I wish to express my sincere thanks to the Weald & Downland Open Air Museum, Singleton, Chichester, West Sussex, who generously allowed me to photograph buildings around their beautiful museum to include in this publication.
All photographs are by Barry Harber or by the author, except for that on page 4 (bottom), which is used by kind permission of Butser Ancient Farm. Those on pages 3, 8, 11, 17 (both), 27 and front cover (bottom left) were taken by Barry Harber by kind permission of the Weald & Downland Open Air Museum, Singleton, Chichester, West Sussex; those on pages 6 and 12 (top) were taken by kind permission of the owner.

Printed in Malta by Gutenberg Press Limited, Gudja Road, Tarxien PLA 19, Malta.

Contents

A low-status timber-framed building built for a family of simple means. (Poplar Cottage, Weald & Downland Open Air Museum.)

Introduction

For thousands of years, ever since man decided to build a shelter in which to live, wattle and daub has been used to construct the walls of people's homes, providing protection against the elements. And it seems incredible that until about 1900 wattle and daub was still commonly used to repair ancient timber-framed structures that survive today.

In the earliest and most primitive form of wattle and daub, wattles (predominantly hazel sticks) were woven around evenly spaced vertical wooden posts set into the ground in

Various thatch and wattle ties, all made from natural materials.

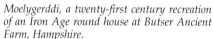

Moelygerddi, a twenty-first century recreation of an Iron Age round house at Butser Ancient Farm, Hampshire.

One of the many ponds created by the extraction of clay to complete wattle and daub infill within a nearby timber-framed building.

circular formation. These formed the walls of the shelter and the techniques used to build them were similar to the way hazel and willow fencing is still made today. Wet clay daub was then smeared on to the wattles, filling in the gaps between the sticks. A conical roof structure, steeply pitched to allow effective shedding of rain water, would then have been erected, the bottom ends of the rafters being tied to the vertical wall posts using natural fibres such as the strong but flexible twisted bark of a young tree or bush. Hazel roof battens would have been tied horizontally around the roof structure joining rafter to rafter, providing a firm framework on which thatch could also be fixed. A good example of a building of this form can be seen at Butser Ancient Farm, Hampshire, where an Iron Age round house that perfectly illustrates the type of structure described has been reconstructed.

Wattle and daub structures were generally built throughout Britain wherever there was a good supply of clay subsoil reasonably close to the site. Extraction of the clay would have left a depression, which often formed a pond, and in many cases the ponds that provided their daub still stand close to

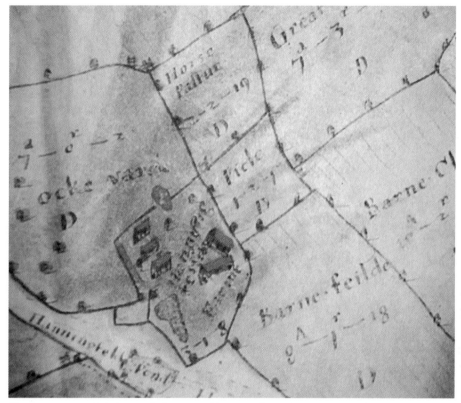

The grey areas marked close to the houses and barns on this early seventeenth-century map illustrate the importance of ponds in the past. There is even a large pond shown in the middle of the road in this village.

timber-framed buildings today. Unfortunately, since about 1950, many of these historic ponds have been filled in, leaving little evidence that they ever existed. Occasionally, the opposite may be the case, where the house has disappeared but the pond still remains, indicating that there was once an old dwelling close by. Where suitable clay subsoil was scarce, builders had to use other materials such as flint or stone and timber-framing is rare.

The structure and make-up of wattle and daub

In certain areas of Britain, beneath the topsoil, lies a layer of heavy clay, formed over millions of years from rock exposed to weathering and erosion, thus creating tiny particles that were buried deeper and deeper as more and more sediment was deposited on top, either on the ocean floor or on river beds. However, as a result of plate tectonics (the movement of continental areas over the surface of the globe) and continually rising and receding sea levels, much of this sediment, which we know as clay, is on dry land today and easily accessible. Different areas of Britain produce different coloured clays, depending upon the rock from which they were formed, and much clay contains lumps of white chalk, a type of limestone, formed over millions of years from the shells of dead marine creatures.

This excavation reveals the lighter clay layer clearly visible just beneath the darker topsoil.

Clay interspersed with lumps of white chalk.

Interwoven hazel
wattles like these are
still used for fencing
today.

A heavy, sticky clay interspersed with chalk is the ideal material to create daub. Combined with water, or perhaps in the past animal urine, together with organic matter such as dried grass or straw, this would have formed a thick, tacky daub mixture ideal for smearing across an interwoven wattle frame, filling up the gaps between the sticks. Such daub was also used to create whole buildings. The following extract dates from the late eighteenth century and, although it describes the erection of buildings made entirely of clay daub, not wattle and daub or timber-framed, it gives a picture of how things might have been done throughout Britain in the past:

> Then they procure from a pit contiguous... as much clay or brick earth as is sufficient to form the walls, and having provided a quantity of straw or other litter to mix with the clay, upon a day appointed, the whole neighbourhood, male and female, ... assemble, each with a dung fork, a spade or some such instrument. Some fall to working the clay or mud by mixing it with straw; others carry the materials; and 4 or 6 of the most experienced hands build, and take care of the walls. In this manner the walls of the house are finished in a few hours after which they retire to a good dinner and plenty of drink which is provided for them, where they have music and a dance, with which they conclude the evening. This they call a daubing. (Sir J. Sinclair, *The First Statistical Account of Scotland*, 1792, pages 22-23).

Today daub is made in exactly the same manner, by treading a similar mix beneath the feet – nowadays shod in wellingtons.

Because the walls of timber-framed buildings are relatively thin (approximately 6 inches or 15 cm), reflecting the width of the structural timbers, the clay daub between each of them needs to be supported by a woven or tied grid of wooden wattles. This wattle grid, which is generally made from sticks of hazel or laths of oak, becomes hidden within the walls once it is

Above left: *The author treading clay daub under foot, a process that has changed little for hundreds of years.*

Above right: *An old woven wattle panel together with some of its clay daub.*

covered both inside and outside with clay daub. These wattles give the daub something to cling to when wet and hold on to once dry. Without the wattle support, clay walls of such thinness might either fall out in one slab or eventually crumble to pieces.

An old wattle and daub panel under repair, with straw, wattles and natural ties clearly visible.

Ancient woodland. Many of Britain's existing woods are at least a thousand years old.

Until just a few hundred years ago, many parts of Britain were still covered in dense woodland. Here underwood, such as hazel, survived and thrived, provided that it was coppiced (cut) about every five to eight years. Coppicing, treating the hazel as a long-term crop, encouraged new growth and kept the rods (hazel sticks) young, straight and flexible – especially important where these were required for weaving. Woven hazel would have been used for a variety of structures in the past, providing not only the walls of houses, but better footing for tracks and walkways, bridges, fencing, the bases of beds and the walls of animal shelters.

It was predominantly hazel that was used to form the wattle support

A healthy hazel stool, the result of regular coppicing, with usable, straight hazel rods of five to seven years growth.

A seventeenth-century wattle-panelled former well house – the Treadwheel House at the Weald & Downland Open Air Museum, Singleton, West Sussex.

grid for the daub walls in houses up to the end of the seventeenth century and it continued to be used even after this period for less important structures around the farmstead.

Originally, flexible hazel wattles were woven horizontally around the upright principal posts sunk into the ground. These posts were arranged in circular formation so that there were no corners to encounter and weaving could be continuous, leaving a gap for an entrance. No ties, nails or fixings of any kind would have been required to make the walls. The wattles relied upon their flexibility to remain in position.

In order to weave successfully with hazel, the wattles were used in their 'green' state, almost immediately after cutting or coppicing and before the sap in the wood could dry out. Once wood has dried to within a certain moisture content, it is said to be seasoned. Using seasoned hazel to weave would have been difficult, because once it has dried it loses much of its flexibility, becoming harder and more rigid with time.

Hazel was used to build many structures in the past. It is slow-growing and has tightly packed growth rings. It is flexible at first but becomes harder as it ages and, as long as it is kept

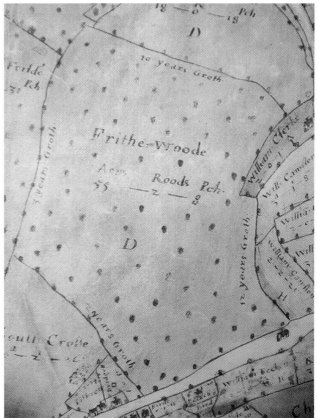

Frithe Wood, over 55 acres (22 hectares) of ancient woodland detailed on an early seventeenth-century map, is thought to predate the Norman Conquest. The name Frithe is said to be derived from the Old English word 'fyrhth' meaning woodland.

dry, it is resistant to beetle or fungal attack. When woven, it makes a sturdy building with enough flexibility to withstand strong winds and slight movement without causing structural problems.

Across Britain today one can still see hazel coppices that

would have been regularly cropped and looked after for hundreds of years, right up to the Second World War. Alas, fifty years of neglect have taken their toll on ancient woodland, which needs regular management if we are not to lose what could still be a valuable, useful and environmentally important crop, still used in thatching and fence-making today.

Old, overgrown and neglected hazel stools within ancient woodland.

From roundhouse to riches: timber-framed buildings became more and more sophisticated as the centuries passed, but wattle and daub has always been used to fill in the spaces between the timbers.

The use of wattle and daub within later timber-framed buildings

Over the centuries timber-framed buildings became more sophisticated, reaching their peak during the fifteenth and sixteenth centuries. Instead of using timbers 'in the round', their natural tree-trunk shape, as would have originally been the case, each timber was skilfully sawn and then trimmed with either an adze or an axe to provide four flat faces. In higher-status homes the exposed faces of ceiling timbers could be carved or roll-moulded to form the most beautiful decoration. Timbers were most commonly put together using a joint called *mortise and tenon* (the mortise being a rectangular hollow and

Beautiful carved and roll-moulded ceiling timbers in a high-status sixteenth-century timber-framed building.

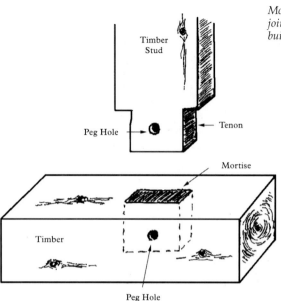

Mortise and tenon – the most common joint found within a timber-framed building.

the tenon being the rectangular tongue that went into the hollow). Roughly rounded (and sometimes even square) wooden pegs would then be driven through smaller, round peg holes, drilled (using an auger) through the mortise and tenon joints of all timbers. These pegs would have locked each joint. Square wooden pegs made for a much tighter fit and because of this were harder to knock through – hence the saying 'like knocking a square peg into a round hole'.

Originally the timber posts of timber-framed buildings were buried and wedged directly into the ground, but in time they would rot away. Later, the timbers were raised up off the earth on a timber sole plate, sometimes also referred to as a sill beam. This plate or beam, which formed the base of the walls of all

Oak pegs like these have for centuries been used to join timbers together.

A square peg in a round (augered) hole.

Below: A pegged joint (mortise and tenon).

later timber-framed buildings, also sat slightly off the ground on a plinth of stone or flint rubble. This prevented rotting of any ground-floor stud work. When brick became more widely available during the fifteenth and sixteenth centuries, the wooden sole plates of timber-framed buildings were raised off the earth on to plinths of brick, although flint rubble continued to be used where this was more easily available or where the timber-framed

A flint rubble and lime mortar plinth beneath a timber sole plate or sill beam.

The holes and grooves which housed the horizontal ledgers within these panels can clearly be seen in the sides of the timber studs in this photograph.

building was of low status. Flint rubble could also be used to stabilise an uneven sole plate.

Instead of weaving wattles around each principal timber post sunk into the ground, a system of holes and slots was cut and drilled into the internal sides (hidden faces) of the timber frame. These holes and slots housed the ends of the wattles, which in turn supported clay daub panels of different shapes and sizes. Timber buildings now displayed their timber frame externally as well as internally and the wattle and daub panels were finished externally with either limewash or lime plaster.

Methods of supporting panels varied across Britain but two types of timber-framed structure are most commonly seen. These are generally referred to as *square panel* and *close studding*.

Square-panel timber-framed buildings display large, wide panels. These are usually square in shape but are sometimes triangular in order to accommodate arched or decorative bracing cutting across a panel. Panels of this shape and size had to be made by the woven wattle method, as woven wattles provide better support for the heavy clay daub in panels that could sometimes measure 3 feet (1 metre) or more in width and height. In order to insert wattles into a square panel, a series of evenly spaced holes were drilled (with an auger) along the middle of the inner face of the upper timber in each panel. A continuous

A fine example of close studding. Lime-plastered infill panels with both timber frame and panels limewashed to finish.

The upright staves and horizontal woven wattles within a square-panelled timber-framed building. These wattles, visible inside this building, would ordinarily have been covered on both sides with daub. (House from Walderton at the Weald & Downland Open Air Museum.)

groove was then cut along the middle of the inner face of the lower timber in each panel. The vertical wattles are called *staves*. It is these that hold the whole panel in the timber frame. Positioned from the top to the bottom of each panel, they were pushed into the augered holes along the top and then tightly sprung into the groove along the bottom of the panel. These vertical staves, which could be of either oak or hazel, were placed with a sufficient gap between them for the wattler to weave horizontally the more flexible, thinner wattles of hazel or

Square-panelled wattle and daub, lime-plastered and limewashed to finish. (Poplar Cottage, Weald & Downland Open Air Museum.)

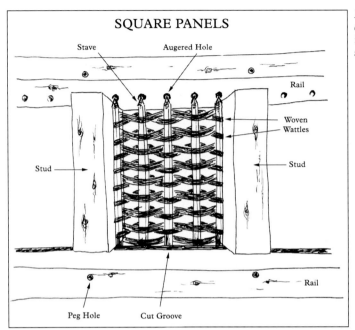

SQUARE PANELS

How wattles are commonly fixed into a timber frame in a square-panel building.

split oak laths. Once the panel was complete, every gap created by each alternately interwoven wattle could be used to key the wet clay daub, helping it remain in place when dry.

Close studding has less space between the upright timbers of the frame and can be seen predominantly throughout East Anglia and Essex. It requires a different method of wattle construction because of the shape of the tall, slim panels. Panels of this type are narrow, commonly about 16 inches (40 cm) in

A wattle groove cut along the top of the sole plate can clearly be seen in this photograph following the removal of the wattle and daub.

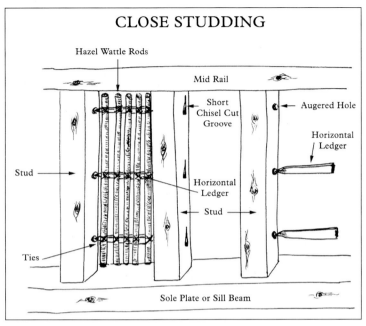

CLOSE STUDDING

Hazel Wattle Rods

Mid Rail

Short Chisel Cut Groove

Augered Hole

Horizontal Ledger

Stud

Horizontal Ledger

Stud

Ties

Sole Plate or Sill Beam

One of several ways in which wattles can be fixed into the timber frame in a close-studded building.

A fine example of close studding. The timbers have been left their natural colour.

The natural twine used to tie these wattles on to the horizontal ledger can clearly be seen.

width, although one can find panels as little as 7 inches (17 cm) wide. Weaving wattles in narrower panels is difficult, and they do not require the support that large square panels with woven wattles demand. Fixing a wattle grid into a close-stud panel is exactly the opposite to the system for a square panel. With close studding the wattles that hold the whole panel into the timber frame (known as *ledgers* in this case) do not run from top to bottom but horizontally from side to side, being sprung into each upright timber (stud) through a system of augered holes one side and short chiselled grooves the other. These holes and short grooves, instead of being cut in the centre of the inner face of each timber as with square panelling, are cut slightly towards the outer face of each timber stud. This allows room for the upright hazel rods to be tied to the ledgers from the inside of a building, keeping the wattle frame in the centre of each panel. Once the horizontal ledgers are wedged in place, usually two or three ledgers to each 6 feet (2 metres) tall panel, whole hazel rods are positioned upright, running from top to bottom. These are fixed on to the ledgers using natural fibres such as natural twine or the strong but flexible twisted bark of a young tree or bush. The upright hazel rods are generally tied a finger's width apart, there being about six to eight rods to each 16 inches (40 cm) wide panel. The gaps between the upright rods allow the wet clay and straw daub to be pushed through and key itself in place.

There are, of course, local variations in construction and it is always fascinating to study old wattle and daub panels to see how creative wattlers could be. Indeed, by studying an old panel prior to repair, one can usually tell whether the panel is original to the building's construction by measuring the amount of shrinkage between timber stud and old clay daub.

Nailed ledgers are another commonly found method of fixing wattles into a timber-framed building.

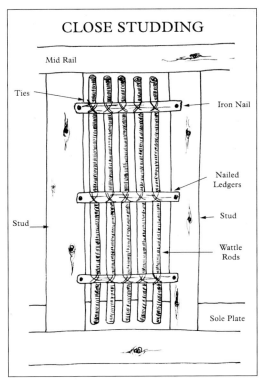

When a timber frame was first erected, centuries ago, the timbers would have been relatively green and full with moisture, pre-dominantly water. Also the newly created wattle and daub panels would have been wet until, with the help of sun and wind and perhaps an open fire within the house, they dried. As the whole timber structure became seasoned, studwork would have reduced in girth, shrinking away from each of the wattle and daub panels. The seasoning of the timbers would have taken several years, larger timbers taking longer to season than smaller. As the wattle and daub panels dried, they too would have shrunk away from the timbers, leaving a considerable shrinkage gap of up to one inch (2.5 cm) in some cases. This is evidence for investigators that a wattle and daub panel is almost certainly an original and not a later replacement. Where a panel is a later replacement (of newer wattle and daub), the shrinkage gap will be considerably smaller, as the timbers will have finished shrinking centuries ago and only the clay daub shrinks away from studwork on drying.

Original shrinkage: the wide gap between the timber stud on the right and the daub panel on the left suggests that both wattle and daub panel and timber frame are original.

Later shrinkage: the narrow gap between the timber stud and the daub panel in this photograph suggests that either the daub is a later replacement or the timber frame has been reused (or perhaps both), which is not uncommon.

When these ancient houses were first erected, builders did not seem bothered by shrinkage gaps surrounding a panel of wattle and daub. They would either have left the gap exposed, particularly where a building was not an inhabited house, such as a brewhouse or kitchen, or lime-plastered over the surface of each panel, hiding the gap from view, but not completely filling it in for comfort's sake, as we might do today. Perhaps when one was exposed daily to strong draughts blowing through unglazed mullion windows, with only ill-fitting wooden shutters for protection, these gaps were of little concern.

Whether square panel or close stud, each wattle panel was daubed with a mixture of clay, straw and water from both sides, inside and out, simultaneously. Where a wattle and daub panel was to be covered with lime plaster to finish, keying holes were made across the surface of the whole daub panel while the clay was still wet. The panel was then left to dry before being lime-plastered. The holes created in the daub provided a key for the lime plaster to hold on to, preventing the plaster from falling off when dry.

Applying wet clay daub with one's bare hands can be a very messy business. However, evidence left in ancient dried daub panels suggests

The red mark seen at the left edge of this lime-plastered wattle and daub panel is telling evidence of the building's (and the panel's) ancient origins. Reddle or ruddle, a natural red earth pigment, was commonly painted on timbers of medieval buildings. In this photograph the ruddle has been deliberately painted over the edge of the timber stud on to the infill panel to make the timbers look wider and thus give the building a higher-status appearance.

Evidence captured in time: this daub fragment from a dilapidated panel displays original float marks made when the clay daub was wet. They appear to have been produced by a small square wooden float used to push wet daub on to wattles. The four indentations shown are no more than 6 inches (15 cm) square.

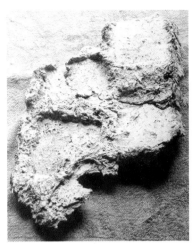

that in the past a type of tool, perhaps a square wooden float with a leather strap handle, was used to push the wet clay and straw mix on to the wattle panels.

Wattle and daub panels of any shape or size can be extremely heavy: the average 'person-sized' panel weighs approximately 20 stone (136 kg) when wet and 10 stone (68 kg) once dry. This is why the wattles which fix the panel into the timber frame need to be firmly wedged in place and not liable to fall out. Provided these are in good condition, a wattle and daub panel will last indefinitely.

It has been said by those who have little regard for this method of ancient construction that wattle and daub is of no importance to the well-being of an old timber-framed building and plays an insignificant part in the structural stability of the timber frame. It is frequently removed during building renovation, generally being replaced with modern building materials that possess none of its unique qualities. But wattle and daub's strengths are at the very least fourfold and are vitally important to the survival of a timber-framed building.

Firstly, merely being securely wedged within the timber frame, wattle and daub possesses a degree of flexibility that allows for slight movement within each individual panel, as buildings of this type, being made from natural materials, are constantly expanding and contracting with the seasons. More

Modern cement render has been plastered over the wattle and daub infill panels of this timber-framed building, trapping moisture and accelerating the decay of both the wattle and daub and the timbers.

Twentieth-century cement render over this timber frame has trapped moisture at ground level and caused premature decay of the mortise and tenon joint of the timber stud and sole plate.

rigid, modern building materials would eventually crack if placed under the sort of pressure of movement that traditional building materials, such as clay and lime, are easily able to withstand over the centuries.

Secondly, wattle and daub is porous. Should water invade a timber-framed building, either rain water entering through render cracks or moisture soaking its way upwards through the base of the walls, which were never built with a damp-proof course, wattle and daub will absorb moisture more readily than the timber frame. Encouraged to dry by the breeze from open windows in summer or by the heat of the house in winter, any build-up of moisture within a wattle and daub panel will evaporate away, leaving the timber frame free from fungus and beetle attack. Wattle and daub panels can be considered the lungs of a timber-framed building. They provide an escape route for moisture that would otherwise permanently damage the timber frame. An excessive build-up of moisture can cause structural movement as the stability of mortise and tenon joints is compromised by decay. Where wattle and daub panels have been removed, moisture ingress, to which every timber-framed building is seasonally subjected, can begin to attack the next available organic material, the timbers.

Thirdly, because of its weight, wattle and daub gives a timber-framed building a certain amount of stability. The average two-bay (three-bedroom) timber-framed house accommodates approximately 13 tons (13,000 kg) of clay and straw within its wattle and daub panels. This affords the skeleton of a timber-framed home a substantial amount of structural support.

Fourthly, wattle and daub panels are built almost flush (in line) with the timber frame. Most panels are between 3 and 4 inches thick (7.5–10 cm) plus about 2 inches (5 cm) externally for render. The centre $1^1/2$ inches (3.7 cm) of each panel is taken up by the wattle framework, the remaining depth either side being clay daub mixed with plenty of straw and perhaps a thin coating of well-haired lime plaster to finish. All of this provides excellent insulation, keeping a timber-framed home cool in summer and warm in winter.

This beautiful thatched timber-framed cottage displays a sunny natural yellow-ochre limewash.

Although many timber-framed buildings were originally designed to display their timbers externally as a show of wealth and status, some buildings were not. Buildings of a lower status or those built for uses other than habitation, such as kitchens or brewhouses, and in particular later built timber-framed homes, may have had their timber frame covered externally when first constructed. Eventually even those timber-framed buildings originally designed to reveal their timber structures externally were plastered over in the following centuries because of changes in fashion and to reduce draughts and provide more comfortable living conditions inside.

Lime render may have been available to wealthier home owners, but a render of nothing more complicated than clay and straw daub may have been normal for many. Indeed, old clay daub renders can been seen on old timber-framed buildings even today and, provided they are well maintained, coated with lime render and regularly painted with limewash only, and not impermeable modern paints, they can last indefinitely.

If a timber-framed building was to be rendered over with either lime-based or clay-based plaster, internally or externally,

A poor little cottage, sadly neglected. Its earthy daub render and nailed wattles are clearly near to falling apart after years without any maintenance.

or both in some instances, the timber frame would need to have been lathed over before the plaster or render was applied. The term 'lath and plaster', which today is used to describe thin wooden laths nailed over a timber frame, coated with lime plaster, is often confused with wattle and daub. This is not surprising, considering that the term could apply to both lime/hair plaster and clay/straw daub plaster. 'Wattle and daub' is generally used to describe the infill situated between the timber studs of a timber-framed building, but clay and straw daub could also be used as a plaster (internally) or a render (externally). Laths of oak or wattles of hazel would have been used to key the plaster on to the timber frame.

Oak laths, long thin strips of wood, were made by splitting green (newly felled) oak logs repeatedly into thinner and thinner strips, the natural fibres of the timber tearing lengthways along the log. Alternatively, and possibly more commonly in the past in lower-status houses, laths made from split hazel rods could be used instead of oak to form a key for plaster, particularly plaster of the less refined, more robust clay and straw daub type. Long hazel rods were also split lengthways, sometimes more than once, depending on the girth of the rod. The split laths, whether made from oak or hazel, would then have been nailed across the timber frame, from stud

Oak laths, long thin strips of wood, were made by splitting a long, green (newly felled) oak log repeatedly into thinner and thinner strips, the natural fibres of the timber tearing lengthways along the log. Oak laths could be used woven within a panel of wattle and daub or nailed flat on walls or ceilings for lath and plaster work.

to stud (on walls), or joist to joist (on ceilings), providing an excellent grip for any render or plaster. In past centuries hand-forged iron nails were used to pin the laths of oak or hazel on to the timber frame and finger-sized gaps left between the laths. These gaps allowed some of the plaster to squeeze through, forming hooks at the back of each lath and enabling the plaster to key itself to the structure. The rest of the plaster or render was then used to cover over the laths completely.

The term 'pargeting' is today commonly used to describe wall or ceiling plaster that has been skilfully decorated with attractive raised or recessed patterns on the surface. Originally this word was applied to any plaster, flat or decorative, used to cover over a surface. Even unseen plaster used to line a chimney flue or undecorative lime or clay render on the outside of any timber-framed building would have been described in the past as 'parge-work'.

A later brick façade cunningly disguises an earlier timber-framed house within. The roof peeking out gives a clue to those who pass by.

The decline in the use of wattle and daub

It is easy to understand why the use of wattle and daub infill declined from the eighteenth century. Brick became more affordable, and timber became scarcer as land was cleared for farming and woodland was not replaced. Brick-built houses multiplied across the country, as the population grew. Many handsome sixteenth-century timber-framed houses were modernised and extended during the Georgian and Victorian periods. Fine timber-framed buildings were completely plastered over with lime inside and out or externally covered in brick, disguising their origins and concealing their 'old-fashioned' wattle and daub panels and timber frame from view. Today, many a timber-framed building hides behind a handsome Georgian brick façade, its tell-tale timber-framed roof unnoticed by those who regularly pass by.

Below: *A lumpy, bumpy ceiling of wattle and daub.*

Many beautiful and historic timber-framed buildings such as these survived for over five hundred years but were demolished after the Second World War.

Wattle and daub continued to be used as a cheaper form of wall or ceiling plaster in less affluent homes and less important buildings until about 1900 but unfortunately its usefulness as a simple but effective infill or rustic plaster for timber-framed buildings appears to have been overlooked.

During the twentieth century, after two world wars and various farming depressions, thousands of buildings throughout Great Britain fell into appalling disrepair. Many rural timber-framed buildings housed tenants who had little incentive or money to repair homes they did not own and such buildings were often simply pulled down and burnt. Those that did survive were sometimes repaired using inappropriate building materials such as modern cement and gypsum plaster, which were relatively new products at the beginning of the twentieth century. Their use on all buildings, new and old, increased mainly because they were easy to apply and they set quickly. But the rigidity and impermeability of cement and gypsum cause premature deterioration of timber-framed buildings and owners of such buildings are beginning to realise that wattle and daub can still be used in exactly the same way as it has been for many centuries. Existing daub, too dilapidated to repair, can be crushed, reconstituted and reapplied, no matter how old the materials. Newly coppiced hazel sticks can be fixed into existing holes, woven or tied to form new wattle panels on which to daub. Clay, dug fresh from

a local source, can be puddled (trodden under foot) together with straw and water for use in repairing old panels or replacing missing ones.

Even in new buildings wattle and daub can easily be used to form the infill panels of twenty-first century timber-framed homes. Its uneven surface can be an interesting feature. Wattle and daub is still a useful, resourceful and plentiful building material, as it has been for thousands of years.

Left and below: New timber-framed buildings erected in 2003 using all of the traditional techniques and materials – green oak with wattle and daub infill.

Wattle and daub infill between the rafters of a thatched timber-framed cottage. Delightful imperfections are part of its charm.

Below: *Wattle and daub can be decorative, being easily moulded by hand or tool to create wonderful patterns around the home. The raised decorative design on this panel of wattle and daub has been created by rolling clay between the palms of one's hands, creating clay 'sausage' shapes. These are gently pressed on to the wet wattle and daub panel in an attractive pattern, pinching the middle of each 'sausage' to keep the pattern slightly raised. Once dry, the whole panel has been given three very thin coats of limewash.*

How to make and repair wattle and daub today

Anyone buying an old timber-framed home today might be forgiven for initially assuming that wattle and daub is such an ancient building material that it could not possibly be of use in the twenty-first century. However, they would be not only wrong but also surprised at how cheap and easy it is to repair.

To begin with, one should always examine a building's method of construction, paying particular attention to how the wattles of the panel are fixed into the timber frame. If the building is 'listed', permission to carry out repairs must be obtained from the local authority and English Heritage. The repairer should then locate a supply of suitable clay as close to the building as possible, as would have been the case centuries ago. If it is not convenient to obtain the clay from land surrounding the house (perhaps the garden is too small), try further afield. For example, neighbours digging footings for extensions to their own homes are usually delighted to dispose of clay subsoil. Once obtained, the clay can be kept indefinitely in a heap outside, uncovered, as frost action over winter breaks the clay up and makes it easier to use, although it can also be used freshly dug.

Next, a supply of hazel rods or oak laths needs to be found and the Forestry Commission's local branch may be the place

A clay store can be kept unprotected outside ready for use.

Hazel wattles can be kept outside until required.

for advice in this respect. Many of them sell hazel coppiced annually from managed woodland and might also know of local sawmills willing to supply green oak for laths. Alternatively, locate an old hazel coppice wood nearby, seek permission from the owner and cut your own.

For the tied method of wattle and daub you will also need to obtain a quantity of natural string, made from either hemp or jute. String produced from natural fibres is much more user-friendly than synthetic products such as baler twine, which is slippery and easily unravels. The string is used only to hold the wattles in place while the panel is being daubed. When the clay daub is dry, the string is of little significance as the clay is pushed through each side, locking itself to the wattle frame. Natural hemp or jute string is generally used today for tying garden plants and can be purchased cheaply from most garden supplies stores. You will also need to obtain straw. Barley or wheat straw will do nicely, although straw grown today bears little resemblance to that used even a hundred years ago, let alone four hundred.

Tying hazel wattles with natural string such as hemp or jute.

Whether or not cow dung was added to any historic daub mix has for many years been deliberated. Having studied and repaired hundreds of wattle and daub panels over the years throughout a variety of timber-framed buildings, the author has never found materials other than clay (interspersed with stones and lumps of chalk) and straw, originally mixed together with water. Wet daub, stored for too long in an airtight container, does indeed begin to smell like the inside of a cowshed and perhaps in past centuries soiled animal bedding could have been incorporated into some daub mixes but it is unlikely that cow dung would ordinarily have been part of a daub mix.

After carefully studying the method of wattling peculiar to your building, replicate it using new hazel wattles or oak laths where necessary, taking great care to repair deteriorated panels rather than knocking them out and replacing them from scratch. No matter how wobbly an old panel may first appear, it is generally a simple matter to insert a new wattle, tie or patch of daub here and there, thus securing the panel for another hundred years.

Where an old wattle and daub panel really is too unstable to repair (perhaps all the wattles have crumbled to dust because of

Below left: *A dilapidated panel of wattle and daub, but not beyond repair.*

Below right: *The same panel after repair and limewashing. A fragment of original ruddle paint has been preserved at the top left of the panel. See the lower photograph on page 22 for a closer view.*

Puddling (treading) wet clay under foot.

Shaking straw into wet clay.

damp or beetle attack), the old clay and straw daub can be carefully removed and placed together with the heap of fresh clay outside ready for incorporation into a new daub mix. The clay heap should remain uncovered as covering may cause mould to grow on the old daub. Old daub can also be kept separately in plastic sacks inside a dry shed, but again the sacks should be left open. To kill any mould growth, expose the daub to plenty of air.

The day before the daub is required for a panel repair or replacement, both new and old clay should be roughly broken up into fist-sized lumps, soaked in water in a wheelbarrow or other watertight vessel, covered with a plastic sheet and left overnight. The plastic sheet prevents too much evaporation of the water, particularly important during hot summer months.

Puddling straw into wet clay.

Turning daub by shovel to ensure a good mix.

When ready to do your mixing, tip the now saturated wet clay on to a flat surface. Begin to tread (puddle) the clay, producing a squashing action with your wellington-clad feet. After a few minutes shake a generous amount of straw on to the squashed clay with one hand while holding on to your shovel with the other. You will need the shovel to turn the mix from time to time and to help steady yourself when treading the daub, as the mixture can become quite slippery.

Repeat the treading underfoot, straw shaking and turning with the shovel three or four times until you can no longer get any more straw into the clay mix and the straw within the mix is completely covered with clay. You may need to add a little water after each straw application to prevent the mix becoming too dry. If you do not add enough straw to the mix (because treading can be exhausting work), you will end up having to make more daub because the straw bulks up the mix to almost double. The straw not only provides better insulation within the finished panels but significantly prevents the surface of the panel cracking up on drying and also helps to hold the whole panel together once the daub has set.

If you are not yet ready to use the wet clay and straw daub, place it in a plastic bucket or bag and keep the air out. It will

Straw within the mix is completely covered in wet clay.

Applying wet daub on to wattles with rubber-gloved hands.

keep well for at least a month if kept airtight. (This is the opposite to how you should treat dried daub, which needs air to prevent mould.)

By this stage, you should have a wattled panel ready to daub and it is a simple, if energetic, task to apply the wet clay and straw mix by getting handfuls of the daub and pushing them firmly on to and between each of the wattles, filling up all of the gaps. On a major restoration project, perhaps where the outer render has been completely removed, you might have access to both sides of a panel, from both inside and outside of the house. However, many restorers may have access to a panel from only one side of the building, generally the inside, and this makes repairs to the panels less easy.

Once enough daub has been applied to the wattles, the clay should be smoothed over using a builder's metal float or even just your rubber-gloved hands. If the panel is to be limewashed when it has dried, the daub can be finished flush with the timber frame, although the surface will still shrink back slightly on drying. If the panel is to receive a coat of lime plaster on top, the daub surface will need to be recessed about half an inch or one centimetre from the surrounding timber frame to allow for the depth of plaster. The daub surface will also need to be keyed (when the clay is wet) with dozens of downward-pointing holes the size of your little finger. These keying holes, which

Wattles ready to daub.

Keying holes made across the surface of new wattle and daub panels ready for lime-plastering.

should be made with a small wooden stick (not your little finger), provide excellent grip for the lime plaster and have been used successfully for hundreds of years to key lime plaster to daub panels.

When repairing an old, perhaps even an original wattle and daub panel, it is important to remember how very dry the clay and straw daub may have become over the centuries. In order to key (stick) the newly mixed wet daub successfully to the old dry panel, without a crack developing between the two on drying, it is important to spray the surface of the old daub thoroughly and heavily with water before repair. New, wet daub should then be carefully but firmly pressed into or on to the old daub where necessary, and the surface finished off slightly proud of the existing daub, as the newer daub will shrink back a little on drying.

It is an extremely satisfying and rewarding experience to repair an ancient and sometimes original wattle and daub panel. Unfortunately, throughout the twentieth century and even during the twenty-first, many of our oldest surviving timber-framed buildings have had their wattle and daub panels removed and replaced with inappropriate substitutes. This book has been written to bring about better understanding and appreciation of wattle and daub and to encourage its greater use in the future.

Further reading

Atkinson, David. *Weathering, Slopes and Landforms*. Hodder & Stoughton, 2004.
Barnwell, P. S., and Adams, A. T. *The House Within*. HMSO, 1995.
Brown, R. J. *Timber-Framed Buildings of England*. Robert Hale, 1997.
Brunskill, R. W. *Timber Building in Britain*. Gollancz, 1994.
Cunnington, P. *How Old Is Your House?* Alphabooks, 1988.
Grenville, J. *Medieval Housing*. Leicester University Press, 1999.
Harris, Richard. *Discovering Timber-Framed Buildings*. Shire, third edition 1993; reprinted 2004.
Hurd, J., and Gourley, B. *Terra Britannica*. James & James, 2000.
Iredale, David, and Barrett, John. *Discovering Your Old House*. Shire, fourth edition 2002.
McCann, John. *Clay and Cob Buildings*. Shire, third edition 2004.
National Trust. *Guildhall of Corpus Christi, Lavenham*. National Trust, 2004.
Quiney, Anthony. *The Traditional Buildings of England*. Thames & Hudson, 1995.
Pritchett, I. *The Building Conservation Directory*. Cathedral Communications, 2001.
Rackham, O. *The History of the Countryside*. Phoenix-Orion Books, 1997.
Sunshine, Paula. *You've Been Timber-Framed!* Barry Harber PR, 2003.
Toghill, Peter. *The Geology of Britain: An Introduction*. Airlife Publishing, 2005.

Places to visit

Avoncroft Museum of Historic Buildings, Stoke Heath, Bromsgrove, Worcestershire B60 4JR. Telephone: 01527 831363. Website: www.avoncroft.org.uk
Butser Ancient Farm, Chalton, near Petersfield, Hampshire. Telephone: 023 9259 8838. Website: www.butser.org.uk
Chiltern Open Air Museum, Newland Park, Gorelands Lane, Chalfont St Giles, Buckinghamshire HP8 4AB. Telephone: 01494 871117. Website: www.coam.org.uk
Museum of East Anglian Life, Stowmarket, Suffolk IP14 1DL. Telephone: 01449 612229. Website: www.eastanglianlife.org.uk
Museum of London, 150 London Wall, London EC2Y 5HN. Telephone: 0870 444 3852. Website: www.museumoflondon.org.uk The medieval galleries include a recreation of a section of wattle and daub
The Weald & Downland Open Air Museum, Singleton, Chichester, West Sussex PO18 0EU. Telephone: 01243 811363. Website: www.wealddown.co.uk
West Stow Country Park and Anglo-Saxon Village, The Visitor Centre, Icklingham Road, West Stow, Bury St Edmunds, Suffolk IP28 6HG. Telephone: 01284 728718. Website: www.stedmundsbury.gov.uk

Index